DAY OF THE DIESELS
Volume 2: 1975-79

DAY OF THE DIESELS
Volume 2: 1975-79

John Spencer Gilks

Edited by Mike Esau

· RAILWAY HERITAGE ·
from
The NOSTALGIA Collection

First published in 2006

British Library Cataloguing in Publication Data

A catalogue record for this book is available from the British Library.

ISBN 1 85794 246 9
ISBN 978 1 85794 246 0

Silver Link Publishing Ltd
The Trundle
Ringstead Road
Great Addington
Kettering
Northants NN14 4BW

Tel/Fax: 01536 330588
email: sales@nostalgiacollection.com
Website: www.nostalgiacollection.com

The number appended to each caption is the negative number. Requests for prints may be made via the Publishers.

Printed and bound in Great Britain

Half title **Buckton Lane Crossing, Bempton, Humberside; Class 40 No 40084, 11.12am King's Cross-Scarborough via Bridlington, 3 July 1976.**
It is less than two years since I acquired my present home and I am using it as a base for a few days' leave. The lady crossing-keeper has just come out in her pinafore to open the gate for the train of the week. Ken Dodd helped to save this line from closure, but usually DMUs between Hull and Scarborough were the order of the day. *6426*

Page 2 **Commercial Road, Weymouth, Dorset; Class 33, 15.45 boat train from Channel Islands to Waterloo being led from quay through street to main line, 15 May 1976.**
Do notice the parking restrictions painted on the road and the two linesmen prepared to halt any approaching vehicles. On 11 July 1960 I stood at the junction of Commercial Road, George Street and Western Road to watch this train – steam-hauled by No 1363 – cross the intersection, creating traffic chaos even then, and recording the event for the BBC *On Railways* programme. The result was transmitted on 23 October 1960. On 3 September 1983 the 'Talking of Trains' (Surbiton) class chartered the saloon that had carried Prince Charles and Lady Diana to Romsey on their wedding day, and had it coupled to the boat train as a present for me for being with them for more than 20 years – a very happy gesture. Gavin Mist was responsible for ensuring that I looked south at Clapham Junction so that we didn't see the saloon until arriving at Waterloo station! *962*

Title page **Milton, Cumbria; Class 37, freight 8M59 heads west from Newcastle to Carlisle, 16 May 1976.**
This is the nearest location to my favourite hotel, Farlam Hall. The bridge was inaccessible a couple of months ago due to flood water. *7752*

Top left **Ings Lane, Hensall, North Yorks; DMU, 14.55 Doncaster-York, 27 June 1975.**
I've brought my car here as I assumed, wrongly, that the proposed Selby Diversion of the East Coast Main Line would start here and I wanted a picture before construction work began. In the event it was about a mile further north! This was my last car to be given a numerical Surrey registration, car number six, as such work was transferred to Swansea. *5495*

Middle left The author on a seat at Llanfihangel Crucorney, Gwent, bequeathed to the memory of John Beardsmore 'who walked the lanes and watched the trains', photographed by Trevor Owen on 4 June 2003.

Bottom left The editor, Mike Esau, pictured by the author at Nawton working on this book in the autumn of 2005.

Right **Gerrards Cross, Bucks; Class 47, 07.13 Birmingham (New Street)-Paddington, Saturday 18 March 1978.**
The train prepares to negotiate the platform road as the signal box is switched out. I am here on a 'Talking of Trains' class visit by coach. The site is to become infamous for the collapse of the tunnel being built to support a Tesco supermarket in 2005. *2304*

CONTENTS

Crofton Curve, Wilts; Class 47 No 47079, Olympia-Newton Abbot Motorail, 9 August 1975.
When the GWR set out to shorten its route to the West Country by providing a main line through Westbury, it had to use the former Berks & Hants line for some distance and could do little to improve the curve resulting from the location of the adjacent canal and the site of Crofton Pump House. Hence the speed restriction on this train as it negotiates the bend in the upper picture.

As it heads west we can see on the left the remains of the Crofton East Curve, built in 1905 to facilitate access to the new Tidworth military camp. Just round the corner it joined the Midland & South Western Junction Railway (Andover to Cheltenham). The cant of the track meant that coming north a train on the spur tilted one way, then the other. I well recall my only journey (from Easton to Paddington on 'The Docks Express' on 16 September 1956) over the curve during dinner, which resulted in my pork chop and vegetables sliding about the plate! The curve was taken out of use the following year. *1698/1699*

INTRODUCTION

As promised in the Introduction to *Day of the Diesels* Volume 1, here is the sixth book in what has become a kind of series, and for new readers I feel I owe some explanation of the origin of the pictures and text.

There are three main strands. First was my intention to explore the entire British Railways network as it existed in the mid-1950s when I was in my 20s. If the passenger service had been withdrawn from a branch line or cross-country route, then permits were obtained from BR, generously given and with only one notable unreasonable refusal –which was overcome – to travel on the surviving goods train. This led to a developing interest in the organisation. Often I travelled with Harry Grenside and Alan Lillywhite – 'three men in a train', as it were. Having observed vantage points for photographs, I returned by car with my camera, and these pictures illustrate magazines to this day.

Second was my setting up in 1960 in Surbiton in Surrey of an adult education class ultimately under the title 'Talking of Trains', which still meets most Wednesday evenings under its third tutor. This led to annual dinners, coach outings to photograph trains, special charter trains, including some in General Managers' saloons, and weekend schools. It so happened that the son of one of the promoters of the class became Chief Commercial Manager of BR, with obvious benefits. Sadly he is no longer with us. I now run a group brought together by personal invitation in Malton in North Yorkshire, which is gradually developing into an authoritative club.

And third, in my professional life with the Association of District Councils, I was responsible for quarterly meetings with the Chairman and top brass of British Rail in the late 1970s and early 1980s, where matters of mutual concern were discussed and some problems solved. This gave me further insight into the organisation of railways.

In the last book I drew attention to pages 303/314 of Andrew Marr's book *Ruling Britannia* (Michael Joseph, 1995) where he sets out how the road lobby, in the modern form of Road Construction Units, superseded the railway monopoly by legislation effective from 1 April 1937. I am fascinated by watching the balance between rail and road. I really believe that in the latest 'Freightmaster' (Winter 2006) there are more companies and trains devoted to the movement of railfreight than hitherto. Certainly more people are voting with their feet and passenger trains are filling up – we even need more coaches! People are also becoming aware of ticket competition. I was fascinated recently to find that by intelligent use of the internet I could travel between York and London first class for less than half the price of the recognised fare – and on the train I wanted to use each way. I shall spend the surplus on lunch. So privatisation is settling down at last, but it has a long way to go to recapture the expertise of BR that was so wantonly wasted both financially and in human terms.

However, the situation at Norton Bridge station in Staffordshire should be a warning to us. I have visited the site more than once in the last 12 months. Table 68 of the National Rail Timetable shows that buses have replaced trains between Stafford and Stoke on Trent. None of the intermediate stations have been officially closed; as far as I know no proposals have yet been submitted to the appropriate TUCC, assuming that they still have the power to intervene. Yet the footbridge to the island platform at Norton Bridge has already been removed, so it is inaccessible even though the nameboards still stand on the platform. On 23 July 2005 the environment there was an absolute disgrace. Piles of redundant steel fencing had been dumped willy nilly into the parking area, there was no word about the 'withdrawal' of passenger trains, and no indication of the whereabouts of the substitute bus. At Stone station (which has won various awards) is the usual timetable board for trains, but it was only by consulting a piece of paper wrapped round a lamp-post that I discovered the bus called only at the end of the station approach. This is not good enough in 2005. I believe that access for the disabled is causing a problem with reaching the far platform, but sympathetic as I am to the handicapped, the able-bodied majority should not be inconvenienced in this way.

It only remains at this stage to set out the principles that guide the text. The caption to each picture begins with its location on the Ordnance Survey map (using station names from 1955 and local government areas as in April 1974 – thus Humberside survives), then details of the locomotive and its train, and the date of the photograph. The number at the end relates to the colour slide from which the black and white print is produced.

Finally may I close here by thanking Peter Townsend for promoting the book, Mike Esau for his editing abilities, and Will Adams and Mick Sanders for designing and laying out the book. As usual John Edgington has put me on the right lines, and Mrs Terry Stevens has jolted my memory. The logo is designed by Gavin Mist.

John Gilks
Nawton, 2006

Retford, Notts; Class 55 No 55008 *The Green Howards*, 13.00 King's Cross-Edinburgh, 30 September 1976.
On the up platform is a plaque commemorating the WRVS and wartime teas. I travelled on the blue prototype 'Deltic' on 18 September 1959 from London to Doncaster to record sounds for the BBC, but the noise was so terrific that the tapes couldn't be used! *5433*

1.
SOUTH AND WEST

Anyone returning to the South London area after many years abroad would find the railway network much as when they left. Although house-building tended to follow the lines and there was much confusion between 19th-century rival companies as to who should build exactly where, which has bequeathed a bit of a muddle in getting to London terminals, nevertheless the basis has proved resilient and can compete with the increasing congestion on the streets. With hindsight the companies were fortunate in buying substantial acreages when land was comparatively cheap. Indeed, some might say that house prices have been one result of their success.

We have much to thank Sir Herbert Walker, General Manager of the Southern in the 1920s, for his far-sightedness in electrification. Equally important was his company's policy that trains from branch lines should run beyond their junction with the major route. Folk from Bromley North do not normally have to change at Grove Park, nor those from Tattenham Corner at Purley – unlike other companies, which insisted that travellers from St Albans, for instance, should change at Hatfield (without the benefit of pre-war electrification) or from Staines at West Drayton. I have been delighted to see that in recent times trains to and from Uckfield start in London and on weekdays do not involve a change at Oxted. This follows the best tradition and seems to have gone unnoticed.

I was born and lived for more than 50 years in Kingston upon Thames. Inevitably, therefore, my early pictures are concentrated in the south. But one picture I never managed to obtain was a train crossing from the St Helier line to the South Western main line near Wimbledon. My editor, Mike Esau, put this right on 26 May 2004 when he pictured 'The Sunny South Special' with No 73096. I have in mind to convert this to a slide so that everyone can enjoy it.

Another train that always intrigued me was the 5.42pm Paddington-Birmingham (New Street) and the equivalent up train at 7.13am. It was the only 'proper' train to survive, and the only one each weekday between Old Oak Common and Northolt Junction (via Greenford). On Saturdays it ran via the Greenford Loop (see pages 27-28). I travelled on it to Birmingham one summer evening and was amused to find empty brandy/whisky glasses in every 1st Class compartment after commuters had alighted at High Wycombe To guarantee drivers' familiarity with the route there is still a train over the section; currently it is the 11.28 Princes Risborough-Paddington and the 12.55pm return, which run only on Mondays, Tuesdays, Thursdays and Fridays!

Under the picture of Whitchurch North (page 16) I remark on the Longparish line in Hampshire. It runs through an up-market neighbourhood, and survived between there and Fullerton Junction until 1956, used for wagon storage. Perhaps this is why on Sundays a visitor could hear the sound of circular saws tearing through wood as the trucks became flat wagons. When the authorities eventually came to remove them there could not have been much woodwork in evidence. I recall discussing wagon storage with the Director (Freight) of British Rail. He commented that the government had never made firm its intentions as regard the movement of freight. When much of this transferred to road haulage, BR didn't know whether or not to scrap the wagon fleet. So it stored much of it. I recall the line between Quainton Road and Verney Junction, where miles of wagons stood silent. They had to be divided to allow access to farm crossings and footpaths! Another was the up line between Olney and Turvey. Eventually the position developed as today, when block workings with coupled sets of vehicles are the norm.

There are two visits I might highlight before beginning this section. David Stonor suggested that before electrification took place we should photograph the Midland main line between St Pancras and Bedford. This was a good idea, so we took the car from bridge to bridge on 2 July 1977 and finished the work on 3 June 1978. Similarly we then followed the Great Western from London to Reading on two dates in 1978 – 29 July and 16 September. I hope you enjoy some of the results and the other views that follow.

Latchmere Junction, London SW11; Class 33, northbound freight from Brighton line, 26 July 1975.

This picture is taken from the roof of Torrington House, Yelverton Road, SW11. I had blithely said at the 'Talking of Trains' class that I could find no locations to photograph the West London Extension Railway. David Pickett, one of the members, then approached the GLC and arranged for three of us to ascend the vertical metal staircase to the roof of these premises – a superb view. You can see to the right of the train the connection to the Windsor side of Clapham Junction; the train itself is coming from the south side, and ahead runs the line that brings trains to Herne Hill (and also in recent years the Eurostars from their depot at Old Oak Common to the platforms at Waterloo via a spur that can be seen disused at the top of the photo). 21

Above Albury Heath, Surrey; 'Tadpole' DMU, 14.49 Tonbridge-Reading, 7 May 1978.

Plenty of watercress growing hereabouts! These 'Tadpole' units were two coaches from a narrow ex-'Hastings' set and a conventional coach. The line between Reading and Redhill has seen a transformation in traffic flow in recent years; it was very down-at-heel when this picture was taken, but then Gatwick Airport opened and an hourly express service from there, reversing in Redhill, now augments the local trains. *420*

Below Botley, Hants; Class 33, 11.05 Eastleigh-Fareham, 7 October 1978.

Although my timetable researches suggest that this is the train described above, I am suspicious as the stock looks more important than that (perhaps Reading-Brighton?). On the right of the island platform can be traced the remains of the Bishops Waltham branch, which lost its passenger service as long ago as 1933. I travelled on the goods train on 12 March 1955 and the relaxed regime permitted it to pause at Durley Halt for a photograph of the crew and other members of the Railway Enthusiasts Club. Goods traffic ceased in 1962. 633

Above Beaulieu Road, Hants; Class 33, 07.02 Newcastle-Poole,
7 October 1978.
Only a handful of trains (three down on Monday to Friday for
example) currently call at this lonely station in the New Forest, but at
the heyday of electrification it could boast an hourly service. It is 4
miles from Beaulieu – the word 'Road' in a station name has always
been a warning to travellers. 836

Below Lockerley, Hants; Class 33s, 13.58 Exeter (St David's)-
Brighton, 2 June 1979.
A day out in the car with Gavin took us to the Reading/Basingstoke
line, Alresford, the Wylye Valley and the GW main line. 989

Above East Dean, Hants; Class 47, 08.00 Cardiff Central-Portsmouth Harbour, 20 April 1975.
The location is between Dean and Dunbridge stations. Along this section two sidings diverged to the south, one to a military depot and the other to a quarry. Until 1964 Alderbury Junction gave access to the line to Fordingbridge and Wimborne. *990*

Below Near Groveley earthworks, Wilts; Class 31, 12.07 Portsmouth Harbour-Bristol (Temple Meads), 2 June 1979.
We are in the lovely Wylye Valley now, and this train is just accelerating away from the speed restriction that governs the north-to-west curve behind the hill. All the wayside stations here closed in 1955, when I cycled from Salisbury to Warminster to capture them on film. *1035*

West Dean Farm, Wilts; DEMU, 11.45 Salisbury-Portsmouth Harbour, 20 April 1975.

In order to provide a page for this lovely view, the pictures are slightly out of geographical order. We are just inside the eastern border of the county, and I am waiting for David Shepherd's steam engine to pass with a charter special. 998

Commercial Road, Weymouth, Dorset; Class 33, 15.45 Weymouth Quay-Waterloo, 15 May 1976.
This train proceeded so cautiously that it was not difficult to obtain more than one photograph (see also page 2). 963

Above **Whitchurch North, Hants; Class 33, 09.56 Reading-Salisbury, 26 March 1977.**
This was our first stop on the 1977 'Talking of Trains' coach tour. Subsequently we photographed trains at Hurstbourne, Hungerford, Combe Halt, Heyford, Ardley, Quainton Road, Cheddington, Ampthill, Millbrook and Ashwell & Morden, finishing with fish and chips at Baldock. What wonderful days they were! The up island platform originates with the branch from Hurstbourne to Fullerton Junction on the Test Valley line opened in 1885 and closed to Longparish in 1934 (beyond there in 1956). *1018*

Below **Near Tisbury, Wilts; 'Hastings' DMU, 09.00 Brighton-Exeter (St David's), 22 March 1975.**
These narrow units were later superseded (see page 11). It so happens that this photograph was taken on the 1975 coach tour, which had stopped first at Micheldever and Wylye and later at Dundas Aqueduct, Patchway, Sapperton, Charlbury, Bletchington and Blackthorn. *1067*

Above Semley, Dorset; Class 33, 10.08 Exeter (St David's)-Waterloo, 22 March 1975.
The coach has stopped again. It's obvious that rationalisation is in progress, the station having closed in 1966. Southern Railway timetables show bus connections with Shaftesbury, now linked to Gillingham further west. *1072*

Below Maiden Newton, Dorset; DMU set B801, 12.15 Weymouth-Bristol (Temple Meads), date uncertain.
Until 1975, in the days of diesel railcars, the up island platform bay was used by trains for Bridport. Hitherto the steam engine retreated while its coaches were fly-shunted into the platform. Now the station boasts just a loop on the single line from Yeovil to Dorchester. *1092*

Welwyn Tunnels, Herts; Class 47, up express, date unknown.
The lack of details is not very commendable, but I hope you find the picture of interest! When I visited King's Cross signal box in the 1980s my one question was how far north did an up express have to be so as not to be delayed by a local using the double-track section from Woolmer Green Junction and calling at Welwyn North Station. No one seemed to know. No wonder the express is often checked as far back as Hitchin! *5343*

St Paul's Road Junction, London NW1; DMU, 10.05 St Pancras-Luton, 2 July 1977.
The next 11 pictures were taken on two visits with David Stonor to the Midland main line prior to the erection of masts for electrification as far as Bedford and before the semaphore signals were taken down. It proved to be a good idea – we visited nearly every over-bridge and other vantage points. This picture is taken at the point at which the service now known as Thameslink diverges (left) to run largely underground as far as Blackfriars. These lines were in use for a service to Moorgate in July 1868, some three months before the terminus opened. The North London Line runs overhead in the background. *4783*

Above West Hampstead, London NW6; Class 47, 08.27
Nottingham (Midland)-St Pancras, and up local DMU, 2 July 1977.
From time to time it has been suggested that there should be a multi-million-pound interchange here, for there is a station nearby on the Metropolitan Line and another served by the Richmond-North Woolwich trains, but nothing ever happens! The goods lines on the left carry traffic from, say, Dalston to Neasden. *4792*

Below Cricklewood, London NW2; Class 45, 09.00 Sheffield-St Pancras, 2 July 1977.
What a wonderful array of signals! Those on the gantry (far left) handle the junction for Neasden and Acton Wells by way of a triangle with tracks from the north, which we shall see overleaf. We are standing on the up local platform. *4804*

Above **Brent Viaduct, London NW4; Class 47 No 47490, 12.01 St Pancras-Sheffield, 2 July 1977.**
The North Circular Road passes under the railway here at Staples Corner as the M1 begins its journey north to the left on the other side. The 19th-century brickwork of the railway viaduct contrasts with more modern materials. *4807*

Below **Near Silkstream Junction, Hendon, London NW4; Class 45, 13.01 St Pancras-Sheffield, 2 July 1977.**
The goods lines on the right are rising to cross the main and local lines to join the latter at Silkstream Junction, where the six running lines are thus reduced to four. A spur connects the goods lines to the main line. The local lines on the left, dividing as they approach the junction, are adjacent to the then new M1 extension. *4814*

Right Elstree & Borehamwood, Herts; Class 45,
14.01 St Pancras-Sheffield, 2 July 1977.
The train leaves Greater London and enters Hertfordshire in Elstree
Tunnel. We were concerned lest electrification meant the destruction
of this fine iron colonnade. *4817*

Below Red Road, Elstree, Herts; Class 45, up parcels,
2 July 1977.
See how lofty the semaphore signals have to be so that the driver of an
approaching train can see them without hindrance from the bridge;
they have co-acting arms below. A Saturday train exclusively for
parcels is probably a rarity now. I have never understood why the
authorities don't take more advantage of the coupling together of
passenger and freight vehicles now that riding qualities have improved
so that a reasonable speed can be maintained. Perhaps separate
accounts are required! *4822*

Above Radlett, Herts; Class 47, empty stock to Cricklewood, 2 July 1977.
A delightful scene that speaks for itself! *4827*

Below Harpenden, Herts; Class 45, 13.12 Nottingham-St Pancras, 3 June 1978.
The co-acting double-arm signal adds interest to the scene, and in the background are the distants for the down slow to down main connection at Harpenden Junction, where the Hemel Hempstead branch headed west. The branch was closed to passenger traffic in 1947 and to freight hereabouts in 1964, and I travelled the branch with the goods on 10 March 1956. There was also a northern spur at the junction for 11 years until 1888. The track layout suggests that the local lines were added later. This is a station much frequented by commuters. *4840*

Above Sundon, Beds; Class 45, 13.00 Sheffield-St Pancras,
3 June 1978.
We are now beyond Luton. Just north of here the M1 almost touches
the main line, and for years motorists could see a range of lower-
quadrant Midland Railway signals. *4859*

Below Elstow, Beds; Class 47, empty stock, Leicester-
Cricklewood (ex-Scarborough holiday train), 3 June 1978.
The tall chimneys mark the London Brick Company's premises. David
and I continued our photography as far as Kempston Road Junction,
Bedford (electrification has not yet continued north), then returned to
a restaurant in Ampthill for dinner before going home. *4863*

I am on the 'Talking of Trains' coach tour that first called at Gerrards Cross, and since then we have been to Chesham and Tring. We shall go on to Souldrop, Glendon Junction, Harringworth Viaduct, Oakham, the Nene Valley Railway, Abbots Ripton, Royston and Ware! The Bletchley-Bedford section is virtually all that remains of the Oxford-Cambridge line and has recently been modernised. The M1 bridge is behind the train. Do notice the original level crossing gates. *3821*

Northolt Junction, South Ruislip, Greater London; DMU, 10.25 Marylebone-High Wycombe, 29 July 1978.
When the Great Central & Great Western Joint Line was constructed between here and Ashenden Junction in north Bucks in 1906/1910, the intention was that Paddington trains should have an unchecked run here, and GC trains at the northern end. In the event, history has dictated that there are only four scheduled passenger trains each week to and from Paddington (on a formation reduced to a single track), while the Marylebone trains diverge all day, and at the northern end the GC has shut and the Birmingham service has to slow down. *2294*

Above Adjacent to Ruislip LT Depot, Greater London; DMUs, up Marylebone and down High Wycombe services, 29 July 1978.
I imagine that security measures will have put this bridge out of bounds to other than authorised staff. I believe that the signal gantry in the distance has ended up at the National Railway Museum in York. *2298*

Below Chalfont, Bucks; DMU, 10.10 Marylebone-Aylesbury, 18 March 1978.
Electrification is in place as far as Amersham, where the Metropolitan 'underground' trains turn back. The climb out of the Colne valley to Chorley Wood can be tricky at the time of leaf falls. Until 1966 GC-line expresses ran this way to Nottingham (Victoria), and before that to Manchester and South Yorkshire. On the right is the branch from Chalfont & Latimer to Chesham. *4145*

Above Ranelagh Bridge, Paddington, London W2; Class 47
No 47027, 09.48 Paddington-Newquay, 29 July 1978.
Having captured the Midland main line, David Stonor, Keith Bell and
I determined to make a similar pilgrimage to the Great Western
between London and Reading. Again it took two visits. A holiday train
such as that illustrated would not normally leave the principal platform
at Paddington, so it is on the north side of the formation. *1433*

Below Westbourne Park, London W2; Class 47, 10.23
Paddington-Paignton, 29 July 1978.
The Hammersmith & City tracks cross beneath the former GWR main
line here. A westbound LT set and a DMU (probably to Slough) are
about to be overtaken by the express. *1443*

Above Ealing Broadway, London W5; Class 33s, relief to 08.50
Ripple Lane-Southampton Freightliner, 29 July 1978.
Note that the nearer of the Class 33s is to the 'Hastings' gauge. The
train is emerging from beneath the multi-storey car park. Do also
notice the extra width of the former broad-gauge formation on the left,
and the different widths of the bridges ahead. *1476*

Below West Ealing, London W13; Class 47 No 47024, 08.50
Ripple Lane-Southampton Freightliner, 29 July 1978.
At this point the branch diverges for Greenford and the Birmingham
line of 1910. There is a triangle both here and at the other end, though
most passenger shuttles from Ealing Broadway end up in a bay between
the Central Lines. *1481*

Above West Ealing, London W13; Railcar, 10.25 Ealing Broadway-Greenford, 29 July 1978.

There was a time when the layout of this line enabled a train from Paddington to negotiate the loop clockwise, then climb the connection to Acton Wells Junction and the north, or anti-clockwise and join the West London Line at Old Oak Common and head for Olympia and the south. *1484*

Below Castle Bar Park Halt, London W13; Class 47, 07.13 Birmingham (New Street)-Paddington, 29 July 1978.

As certain signal boxes were switched out on Saturdays, this train did not run via Park Royal but came this way and livened up the branch scene. Waiting passengers are probably quite surprised, but their unit is on the skyline. *1488*

Above Southall shed, Greater London; HST, 11.30 'Cornish Riviera' Paddington-Penzance, 16 September 1978.
Our second visit to the GW main line has begun. The branch to Brentford diverged (right) just here until 1964. *1492*

Below Southall, Greater London; Class 50, 07.50 Paignton-Paddington, 16 September 1978.
Note once more the wide space where the broad gauge used to run. In the background are public utilities for water and gas. *1498*

Above Stockley Road, Greater London; Class 47, 06.15 Penzance-Paddington, 16 September 1978.
This view along the former GWR main line is looking towards West Drayton. *1503*

Below Iver, Bucks; HST No 253019, 08.35 Penzance-Paddington, 16 September 1978.
A photograph of David and Keith taking photographs on the footbridge here is featured in *Trainspotting Days*, also published by Silver Link. *1519*

Above Slough, Berks; Class 47, 01.45 Coatbridge-Millbrook Freightliner two DMUs and a Class 31, 16 September 1978.
This has been a famous station since Queen Victoria made her first train journey – from here to Paddington – on 13 June 1842, Prince Albert and his brother Ernest having preceded her in 1839. The branch to Windsor was not opened until 1849. *1533*

Below Eton Viaduct, Berks; DMU, 12.02 Slough-Windsor & Eton Central, 16 September 1978.
Here is the branch, running over a lengthy masonry viaduct above the meadows before crossing the Thames on a girder bridge. Windsor Castle can be seen clearly in the background. Until 1979 there was also a south-to-west spur at Slough so that the monarch could visit Osborne in the Isle of Wight via Mortimer and Gosport without reversal. *1542*

Above Slough, Berks; Class 50, 12.23 Paddington-Paignton, 16 September 1978.
The Windsor branch curves to the left from its connection with the main line. The Class 08 shunter is one of many serving the industrial estates set up at Slough between the two World Wars. *1545*

Below Ruscombe, Berks; Class 47, Southampton-Ripple Lane Freightliner, 7 July 1979.
Clearly the pre-1892 broad gauge lines used to be on the left, and what the GWR described as the relief lines are on the right, which will lead this train naturally to the incline at Acton to Acton Wells Junction and beyond. *1580*

Twyford, Berks; Unidentified double-headed down express, 7 July 1979.
The station, still the junction for the Henley on Thames branch, is beyond the distant bridge. *1582*

Kingham, Oxon; Class 47s,
16.25 Paddington-Hereford (right) meets
16.25 Hereford-Paddington, 13 May 1979.
Gradually this station has lost its importance, though it still retains double-track on a route otherwise singled over lengthy stretches between Oxford and Worcester. The passenger service to Banbury was cut back to Chipping Norton in 1951 and the remainder was lost in 1962. Then the service to Cheltenham was also withdrawn in 1962. For years a regular Newcastle-Swansea via Barry return through train bypassed the station on an overbridge to the north; it was run to facilitate the transfer of merchant seamen between ships. *2410*

Above Kingham, Oxon; Class 47, 16.25 Hereford-Paddington,
13 May 1979.
The up train seen on the previous page is seen here arriving at the
station. It took 10 minutes longer to get to Paddington than to
Hereford! The grass strip on the right has replaced the tracks for
Banbury. *2413*

Below Near Evenlode, Glos; Class 31, 09.40 empty stock
Worcester (Shrub Hill)-Didcot, 26 April 1975.
The double-track section runs from the level crossing signal box at
Ascott-under-Wychwood to Moreton-in-Marsh. *2452*

Above Near Abbotswood Junction, Worcs; Class 47 No 47446, 14.49 Bristol (Temple Meads)-Glasgow (Central), 13 May 1979.
Just behind me a branch veers away from the main line to serve Worcester, and through trains rejoin near the foot of the Lickey Incline, having passed through Droitwich. *2612*

Below Aynho, Oxon; Class 47, Birmingham (New Street)-Paddington via Oxford, 27 October 1976.
This is the point at which the 'new' line of 1910 parts company with the old and shortens the route to London via Bicester. It is carried by the embankment on the right and the down track has a flying junction with the older formation. British Rail gradually extended the journey of these cross-country trains so that eventually one of them even originated at York! The station here closed in 1964. *2699*

Freshford, Wilts; Class 47, Bournemouth-Swansea holiday train, 9 August 1975. This train and its opposite working ran via Fordingbridge until it closed in 1964. At one time the southbound journey was extended to Pokesdown because there was no room left to accommodate the stock in the resort. A picture of it in steam days (approaching Downton Tunnel) appears on page 133 of Silver Link's *The Nostalgia of Steam* (the 2001 reprint of my *Classic Steam* volume from 1994). 2161

Sapperton Tunnel (south portal), Glos; DMU, 14.45 Swindon-Gloucester (Central), 22 March 1975.
The weather was bleak when I took this photograph and I feel that the atmosphere brings this out. Avid readers will have observed that this is on a coach tour. *2108*

Theale, Berks; Class 47, 08.09 Ripple Lane-Thatcham oil tanks, 17 November 1979.
This is the first of a series of pictures illustrating the GWR's 20th-century main line, until we eventually reach a point west of Plymouth (235 miles from Paddington in the current timetable). *1647*

Aldermaston, Berks; Class 52 'Western, 10.26 Paddington-Paignton (1B45), 2 August 1975.
The down line on the right provides access to Padworth sidings. I'm in the car with the late John and Phyllis Faulkner, and we are going on to the Pendon Museum and Quainton Road, ending up with dinner at The Black Horse, Thame. Although designated Class 5s under the TOPS scheme, all these diesel-hydraulic locomotives had been withdrawn by the time of its implementation. *1653*

Thatcham, Berks; Class 50, 10.58 Paddington-Penzance, 27 August 1979.
The Faulkners' son Frank has joined our company to see trains also at Mortimer, Kintbury, Crofton and Hurstbourne. *1658*

Above Denford Loop, Hungerford, Berks; Class 47, 12.26
Paddington-Paignton (1B65), 23 June 1973.
Please excuse the date – this picture was omitted from the last book!
I've come with the Potter family (Bill was Station Master at Walton on
Thames and later at Reading South) and we are about to have a lovely
picnic by the Kennet & Avon Canal. It is a glorious sunny day. *1684*

Below Bedwyn, Wilts; Class 50, 10.56 Paddington-Penzance,
9 August 1975.
This station marked the boundary between the London and Bristol
divisions. There were no station closures east of here, but none were
left between here and Pewsey by 1966. Hence the local service from
Reading turns back at this point. *1693*

Above Woodborough, Wilts; Class 52 'Western', 10.30 Newquay-Paddington, 9 August 1975.

It's nice to record expansion for a change! There are now up and down loops at this point, and I have seen trains overtake here. It is a fairly remote spot, and the station closed in 1966. *1712*

Below Powderham, Devon; Class 47, 14.25 Paignton-Oxford via Bath (4F70), 28 May 1977.

I have been invited to visit the Starcross Yachting Club in the trees behind the train. I managed some interesting pictures there with trains and boats, but became bored, so absented myself with my camera as the extra holiday trains came along. This one is of particular interest due to its itinerary, including the Foxhall Curve avoiding Didcot. *1831*

Near Dawlish, Devon; Class 47, 12.23 Paddington-Paignton, date unknown.
There have been so many photographs taken here that there is little new to say. I have left the car at Dawlish Warren station, so have quite a long walk back! *1837*

St Germans, Cornwall; HST No 253017, 09.45 Penzance-Paddington, 10 November 1979.
Because of all the curves and gradients, these units could not be used to their full potential, hence the representations to the British Railways Board by the cities of Leicester, Nottingham and Sheffield to have some of them transferred to the Midland main line to replace the aging equipment provided for their people. Local government was successful! *1890*

2.
WALES AND THE MARCHES

When in Wales I always stay at Bryn-y-Fedwen Farm, high opposite the Brecon Beacons with magnificent views, looked after by Mr & Mrs Adams. To reach the Central Wales line I usually follow a lonely road from Llywel to Tirabad through glorious country but under the eyes of the military and near a pseudo-Balkan village.

In recent years my principal visit has taken place in the middle of July, when there is an extra 'proper' train over the Central Wales in connection with the Royal Welsh Agricultural Show. This train was invariably hauled by a Class 37, and in 2005 the rolling-stock consisted in part of the coaches that had operated between two such locomotives over the Settle & Carlisle the year before. The train originates at Rhymney, uses the Swansea Avoiding Line and the Hendy Loop, and calls at Llandovery around 9 o'clock in the morning. It then runs as empty stock from Builth Road to Llandrindod Wells to berth until early evening, when it makes its return run. In 2005 I decided to see it approach the west portal of Sugar Loaf Tunnel, which meant negotiating a forestry road. About half-a-dozen cars were already there; as the train approached the sun appeared and we all cheered! I then made off in pursuit, not realising that I drove at 80mph towards Llanwrtyd Wells, and this concerned me later for I recalled that Trevor Owen had said there was a hidden police trap, rightly on this straight road, in one of the lay-bys. I reached Llandrindod well in front of the special. Its return that day was in splendid sunshine. The show is a week later in 2006, and it remains to be seen whether the special is operated.

On my way to Brecon I usually top up the petrol in Bucknell, where the lady kindly fills the tank. In 2004 she remarked that the Royal Train had gone through that morning but the curtains were drawn and the Queen was nowhere to be seen; she complained that when it returned empty stock the curtains were still drawn – perhaps no one had made the bed! While in South Wales I normally call at the washery at Onllwyn to see the lengthy freight

trains that go there. Trevor and I have sat there for hours awaiting a train, and have been duly rewarded from time to time. There are still places requiring photographs between there and Neath.

Trevor took me to see the Welsh Highland Railway at Caernarfon and we made a return trip with steam as far as the track extends. It proved to be a beautiful day and I can commend a journey there. It reminded me of a time in 1962 (22 May) when I took a picture of No 42601 on a southbound freight at Dinas (as well as at Chwilog, which appears on page 100 of my steam book). The engine had been well polished because shortly beforehand it had hauled a train with Princess Margaret on board. The Welsh Highland has taken over the former standard-gauge trackbed here. I believe my photo was used in some of the company's publicity, but have never seen the result…

I was reminded of happy journeys between Ruabon and Barmouth when travelling in 2005 on the re-opened Llangollen Railway. Malcolm and Margaret Wride and I chanced upon a 'Thomas the Tank Engine' day for our trip from Carrog. The staff seemed well trained and vigilant, but I do wonder whether these stations were built to accommodate so many people en masse, particularly young children, in our less self-disciplined age.

Opposite **Church Stretton, Salop; Class 25, Crewe Works Test Train, 27 August 1976.**
Prior to the August Bank Holiday weekend I'm spending a few days in the Marches and have come across this train as it is being backed into the siding prior to an exchange of locomotives. The buildings on the left are the original station before it was resited on the other side of the bridge in 1914. Both are well located at the end of the High Street.

In the second view the train is heading south, but I cannot say where it terminated. *2861/2863*

Above Caerleon, Gwent; Class 47, 11.30 Cardiff-Crewe, 23 July 1977.
I've driven down the M4 – quite unusual – the previous evening with Mike Cutland and we are staying at The Crown at Whitebrook in the Wye Valley, which is still famous for its excellent cuisine! You will observe that we are passing the day north and east of Newport. *2960*

Below Maindee North Junction, Gwent; Class 47, 08.40 Liverpool (Lime Street)-Paignton, 23 July 1977.
The train has just passed beneath the new M4 and is about to avoid the station at Newport and head direct to the Severn Tunnel and Bristol. Some trains continue to do this today but there seems to be no guarantee that they will always go that way, even when so scheduled! *2962*

Above Magor, Gwent; Class 45, 09.28 Swansea (High Street)-Portsmouth Harbour, 23 July 1977.
We're on the South Wales main line now and the train is heading for the Severn Tunnel. It is one of those extra holiday services that used to run in the summer and is doubtless full of people heading for the Isle of Wight. *2984*

Below Kidwelly, Dyfed; DMU, 10.30 Milford Haven-Swansea (High Street), 12 May 1979.
One of my favourite watering holes was Plas Glansevin at Llangadog, and I often used to spend the weekend there before it became an old people's home. In the dining-room the meal and the wine were first class, while in a barn at the back folk used to come by coach over the hill from the valleys and keep a welcome in song. I always ventured from there to the railways west of Carmarthen, but on this occasion have diverted on the way. *3075*

Carmarthen Junction, Dyfed; Class 47 No 47035, 09.48 Tenby-York, 19 August 1978.
An earlier visit to Plas Glansevin, with Gavin, has brought me here to see this holiday train avoid the station at Carmarthen – not many services do that! When I passed this location in a train last year I noticed that the site is now closed off by a high locked steel gate. *3091*

Sarnau, Dyfed; DMUs, set C613 leading, 10.30 Milford Haven-Swansea (High Street), 19 August 1978.
This is the same working as seen earlier at Kidwelly, but this time photographed from inside the minute signal box that controlled a level crossing until swept away by the installation of an automatic lifting barrier. *3138*

Whitland Tunnel, Dyfed; DMU, 16.10 Pembroke Dock-Swansea (High Street), 19 August 1978.
I'm suspicious about the date because I thought I was alone on this location. A bowstring bridge existed here at a somewhat isolated point and I had called at a farm to ask permission to visit. This was gladly given, with the comment that the bridge had been renewed just that week! *3143*

Tenby, Dyfed; Class 37, empty stock to Swansea of 08.21 from York, 19 August 1978.
The branch from Whitland twists and turns so much through the hilly countryside that it is not difficult to picture the same train more than once. Having done so we now decided to see it leave Tenby over the viaduct at the north end of the station, but to do so we had hurriedly to find our way round a maze of one-way streets. *3154*

Above Lamphey, Dyfed; DMU, 16.10 Pembroke Dock-Swansea (High Street), 12 May 1979.
Here's that afternoon working again deep in the heart of rural countryside. I'm with Mike Cutland again now, and we've come over the new toll bridge from Neyland and the line to Fishguard. According to my diary, wine that evening was Montlouis (white) and Touraine Amboise 1974 (Loire red)! *3167*

Below Clarbeston Road, Dyfed; DMU, 11.15 Swansea (High Street)-Milford Haven, 12 May 1979.
This train provided a connection, at Whitland, with the Paddington-Fishguard express behind, which has come by the Swansea Avoiding Line from Briton Ferry to Llanelli. Until 1964 a steam push-pull unit used to stand in the up bay (at the far end of the platform) to call at all halts to the coast. The priority at the junction – Milford Haven/Fishguard – has varied over the years. *3189*

Cremorne Viaduct, London SW6; Class 33, southbound freight, 26 July 1975.
We have already seen a view from here in black & white (page 10). I'm on the roof of Torrington House, Yelverton Road, SW11. This train has come from beyond Willesden via Olympia and will head for the Brighton line. Chelsea Basin is on the far side of the Thames and the coal yard is now home to expensive apartments. At this time this line was safeguarded by ex-Great Western lower-quadrant signals. 7

Ridgmont, Beds; DMU, Bedford-Bletchley, 18 March 1978.
Again we have been here before (page 24). This time we can see the chimneys of the brickworks that abounded along this line. Until 1968 trains came this way from Oxford to Cambridge. I was advised that had there been a starting signal from the down north bay at Oxford the service might have survived. Its absence meant that trains had to shunt and hang about in such a way that an additional unit was required. At a later date the local authority might have been asked to help financially and, being a specific item, could well have assisted. 3822

Left Harpenden Junction, Herts; Class 45, Nottingham
(Midland)-St Pancras, 3 June 1978.
We're nearer the junction for Hemel Hempstead than on page 22, and
the express is overtaking a goods in the classic fashion. A typical
Victorian masonry arch provides the background. *4846*

Below left South of Narberth (B4315), Dyfed; Class 37
No 37190, 08.21 York-Tenby, 19 August 1978.
We have just seen the empty stock of this train on page 47. This is a
holiday area and I think there is a massive caravan park in the right
background. There used to be a weekday through express from
Paddington to Pembroke Dock, Neyland and Milford Haven titled
'The Pembroke Coast Express'. *3150*

Above Settle, North Yorks; Class 45, Glasgow (Central)-
Nottingham (Midland), 21 May 1977.
A truly rural English scene – the cricketers on the green, the pavilion
and the train. The signal for Settle station box is still in operation.
8664

Right Warmsworth, South Yorks; Class 31, eastbound coal
(9D41), 20 June 1975.
I'm on a bridge west of the A1 motorway, which also leaps across this
massive cutting. Fancy digging it out in the 19th century (1849)! You
can just see the semaphore signal and box in the distance. Hexthorpe
Junction (page 64) is not far behind me. *5449*

Above Battersby, North Yorks; Class 45, Whitby-St Pancras excursion, 28 June 1975.

'K1' Class 2-6-0 No 62005 has brought this train from the coast (and created several lineside fires involving damage to a newly laid signalling cable!). Some American friends asked me why it is still necessary to reverse at Battersby when on the face of it a direct curve north to east could be laid across the field beside this train. My only answer was that they were in England. What a glorious evening! 6867

Below Stainforth & Hatfield, South Yorks; Class 31 No 31155, westbound freight (8T41), 29 March 1975.

Considerable rationalisation has taken place since this visit, but it is still a busy place. It is the junction for the link to the East Coast Main Line at Joan Croft Junction (via Applehurst Junction) and the Leeds line via Skellow and Adwick Junction. I was amused to see that the singer Lesley Garrett appeared on TV recently on the next bridge east of here (adjacent M18) as part of her life story. 6224

Above Reedham, Norfolk; Class 40, empty stock, Lowestoft-Norwich, 6 August 1977.

This is the empty stock of a Liverpool Street-Lowestoft holiday train making its way to the sidings. I wonder where responsibility for opening the swing bridge lies? With the signalman? If so, presumably he has raised the red flag. *5754*

Below Berney Arms, Norfolk; Class 37, Yarmouth-Newcastle, 6 August 1977.

I was determined to see a 'proper' train pass this halt, but to do so Tony Bennett and I had to time it carefully. We boarded a DMU at Reedham and, in accordance with the instructions, asked the guard to advise the driver to stop there. We duly alighted in the pouring rain. Tony is protected by his umbrella, but I had no such luxury and was anxious as the camera was in danger of being damaged. It seemed an age before our DMU returned and we waved it down. The station passenger facilities consisted of a seat, a notice board and a lamp. I wonder whether circumstances have improved? *5758*

Above Broomfleet, Humberside; Class 31, Hull-Doncaster-King's Cross, 29 March 1975.
Since this picture was taken the loops have been removed and the platforms brought forward adjacent to the new formation. I was at the next box east – Crabley Creek – when the Hatfield crash occurred. I was told that that box is kept just for a level crossing adjacent to a farm bordered on the far side by the Humber estuary; it is the best security the farmer can obtain and he is reluctant to allow it to be replaced by a bridge. *6366*

Below Lamberton, Borders; Class 47, Edinburgh (Waverley)-King's Cross, 27 August 1977.
We are just in Scotland and the sea is peeping over the dunes – a good place to be in the sun. *8107*

Above Penmanshiel, Borders; Class 55 'Deltic', Aberdeen-King's Cross, 27 August 1977.

We shall look the other way from the picture in the Scotland section (page 105). Little did I know that the railway and road were to be re-routed northwards here following the tragedy in the tunnel behind the bridge when work was in hand to facilitate the passage of larger containers. A little-known memorial marks the event on the lane climbing on the right of the picture at the edge of the wood. *8174*

Below Dalry, Strathclyde; DMU, Glasgow (St Enoch?)-Stranraer Harbour, 15 May 1975.

The co-acting signals are a joy to behold. Until 1973 trains could diverge south-east at this station and head for Kilmarnock, a line I never travelled or covered with the camera. I wonder why? Before taking this shot I had brought the car from Arran to Ardrossan and I'm going to stay overnight in Cumnock. *9926*

Above Slochd summit, Highland; Class 25, southbound freight, 24 October 1978.

It's been a long climb from Inverness and the locomotive is making quite a noise. But it's nearly there and can ease down to Aviemore. It is very bleak here, but the A9 has become a dual-carriageway in this area. *10892*

Below Drishaig, Strathclyde; Class 27, Glasgow (Queen Street)-Oban, 12 May 1975.

This is the Strath of Orchy and the train is about to run along the shore of Loch Awe. Do notice the low cloud on the mountains – it rained almost all day! *11493*

Spittal Tunnel, Dyfed; Class 47, 09.00 Paddington-Fishguard, 19 August 1978.
No expense was spared by the Great Western Railway in providing a link from London to southern Ireland, with the Badminton route, avoiding Swansea and an alternative to the slow meander via Maenclochog. Now the through train, even on a seasonal basis, has gone – the Class 37 and a set of Mark 2 coaches from Rhymney no longer functions regularly and a two-car DMU from Swansea twice a day – at lunchtime and in the early hours – has to suffice! *3209*

Wolf's Castle, Dyfed; Class 37, 12.12 Swansea (High Street)-Fishguard, 12 May 1979.
This is the down equivalent of the train seen overleaf. We are on the far side of the valley from the next view – much more difficult of access! *3220*

Wolf's Castle, Dyfed; Class 37, 14.58 Fishguard-Swansea (High Street), 12 May 1979.

It must have been very difficult for the railway engineers to find a reasonably level route along the narrow valley of the Western Cleddau River in this neighbourhood, and until recent years double track existed. See how it winds to enter the north end of the defile. I'm standing on the ramparts of an old fort that once guarded the pass. 3216

Above Llanbister Road, Powys; DMUs, set C602 leading, 12.25 Swansea (High Street)-Shrewsbury, 16 July 1977.
The Radnorshire Arms, Presteigne, is my rendezvous with David for this trip. This station used to mark the eastern end of a section of double track from Penybont Junction (see the frontispiece of my *Classic Steam/The Nostalgia of Steam* from Silver Link), along which the tank engines would haul their short express trains at excessive speed. The village is miles away. *3313*

Below Chirk, Clwyd; DMU, 11.25 Chester-Wolverhampton (High Level), 26 April 1975.
I'm standing in England but the train is in Wales, and at the far end of the viaduct is a short tunnel in common with the Llangollen Canal hard by on the right. Freight from Chirk has to run south to Gobowen for the engine to run round before heading for Chester, as there is no crossover in this vicinity. *2793*

Above Chester, Ches; Class 40, 14.42 Llandudno-Manchester (Victoria), 5 June 1976.
At this time there were four tracks along much of the North Wales coast. Now there are two and the Shrewsbury line, single track as far as Wrexham so as to avoid costs for the new main road), diverges in the far distance to the left. *3758*

Below Chester, Ches; Class 25s, westbound cement, 5 June 1976.
The churches of the city stand out above the racecourse in this view to the east. *3762*

Chester, Ches; DMUs, 11.50 from Wolverhampton (High Level), 26 April 1975.
The No 6 signal box (LNWR) stands high above the tracks at the west end of the station. The lines on the left complete the triangle for Birkenhead (Woodside). Through trains from Paddington used to reverse in the station here, hence you could go direct to London from either end of the platforms – Euston or Paddington. 3763

3.
MIDLANDS AND THE NORTH

The loss of the Saturdays-only holiday train is a factor I regret. Obviously the current generation expects to fly abroad or take vacations by car, so there is no demand for the service that used to take people to the coast one Saturday and bring them back a fortnight later.

I mention this subject under this regional heading as the majority of such trains over unusual routes operated here. There must have been some sort of agreement, written or word-of-mouth, between the NUR and NUM that led to the continuance of these services over lines that had long since lost their passenger trains. The Lancashire, Derbyshire & East Coast line (say, Sheffield to Lincoln) is one that immediately springs to mind. A station such as Edwinstowe saw but a handful of trains each year, yet the platforms were in good order. Shirebrook North had its train to and from Skegness. And not only miners – the industrial workers of Leicester found their way to Belgrave Road station where two sets of coaches stood throughout the winter awaiting the weekends when they ventured out to Skegness and Mablethorpe. And some parts of the permanent way between the city and Marefield Junction needed to be seen to be believed! I recall a journey from Boston to Belgrave Road when the train stopped at the long-closed station of Thurnby & Scraptoft. The guard disappeared into the yard and on his return explained that he had been on the public telephone to ensure that the previous train (the only other one!) had been berthed at the terminus before we went ahead. On one occasion I travelled from Lincoln to Halifax by using holiday trains with just one change and only a short wait at Penistone. In the early 1960s BR still based its coaching requirements on meeting the demand of a peak Summer Saturday – the days of public service rather than private profit. Yet it now costs five times as much to run a busy railway as it did

then. How strange! What was the point of all the closures? Where has all the money gone instead?

The LD&ECR has virtually come to an end with the moth-balling of High Marnham Power Station. Previously the section over the Trent to Lincoln had gone, and now much of the remainder is disused. In this section is a series of pictures illustrating the Bank Holiday Monday in 1975 when Midland main line services were diverted via Mansfield. Presumably this has happened quite often, but I am not aware of that fact so I have devoted quite a space to the trains.

I have yet to reach the date when I began regularly to photograph the nuclear flask trains on the Cumbrian Coast line between Sellafield and Carnforth. The vehicles have little interest to me, but the Wednesday service always fascinates and in 2005 I witnessed an occasion when four locomotives were involved – two Class 20s and two Class 37s. The noise of acceleration from a crossing slack was phenomenal. Earlier in the day I had become fearful when encountering dense cloud on the narrow fell road from Duddon Bridge towards Ravenglass, and later water power where a stream meets the River Esk with the incoming tide near Waberthwaite.

The Settle & Carlisle features in my portfolio below, and goes from strength to strength both in freight and tourist terms. In 2005 the Prince of Wales took to the footplate of *Duchess of Sutherland* between Kirkby Stephen and Appleby. He was in the Royal Train when it steamed up Ribblesdale with enormous clouds of black smoke billowing out into the damp landscape. I only just managed to overtake it between Settle Junction and Helwith Bridge thanks to an empty Settle Bypass and a clear run up from Austwick.

Above Droitwich, Hereford & Worcester; Class 47, 17.50
Birmingham (New Street)-Hereford, 20 August 1978.
I find it somewhat odd that a 'proper' train undertook this working, but
I've looked again at the current timetable of that date and there seems
little doubt. Vigilant readers may observe that I am returning from a
Llandadog weekend – it was always pleasant to go home to Kingston
upon Thames via Stratford upon Avon and Banbury. 2626

Below Market Harborough, Leics; Class 47, 16.00 St Pancras-
Sheffield (Midland), 23 September 1979.
Just north of Market Harborough, converging from the right are the
tracks from Northampton and Rugby. Alongside is the surviving line of
the former route to Peterborough and Newark, which terminates at
buffers about 400 yards further on. The last regular trains plied here in
1966. 4933

Above Oakham, Leics; Class 31, 12.36 Birmingham (New Street)-Norwich, 18 March 1978.
We're on our 'Talking of Trains' coach tour, which had its first photographic stop at Gerrards Cross – that seems a long time ago! My first visit to friends living in Oakham was at a time when water there was in short supply and the taps ran dry overnight – also a long time ago. The station is well sited for the town. *4913*

Below Barkston, Lincs; Class 20s, 13.02 Skegness-Derby, 5 August 1978.
There is an element of doubt about the exact date. This train was much photographed at the time and appeared in countless railway journals. It is just passing beneath the East Coast Main Line, having negotiated the junction on the other side and avoiding Grantham (as all such trains do now) to join the tracks to Nottingham. *4269*

Lowdham, Notts; DMU, 07.22 Crewe-Lincoln (St Mark's), 20 June 1975. I often stopped here for a sandwich lunch coming north, and this has proved to be still the case from Nawton going south. En route to Giggleswick I am going to call on Dearn Valley

Coaches at Wath upon Dearne. The owner had attended each week my Transport Studies course at London University, driving down the motorway in his Volvo and returning home by midnight. He deserved the success he achieved at exam time. 4954

Welbeck Colliery Junction, Notts; Class 25, southbound freight probably going to High Marnham Power Station, 20 June 1975.
I'm still on my way to Dearn Valley Coaches. This is the Lancashire, Derbyshire & East Coast Railway (later Great Central), which didn't attain any of its aims and now ends about here with the mothballing of High Marnham, it's last raison d'être. What a pity! An informal agreement (?) between the NUR and NUM ensured the continuance for years of Summer Saturday holiday trains over lines such as this in connection with East Coast resorts. 4333

Shirebrook, Notts; Class 45, 08.00 St Pancras-Glasgow 'Thames-Clyde Express', 31 March 1975.
Easter Monday 1975 saw the diversion of Midland main line expresses via Mansfield, hence this picture. I spent much of the day between here and the junction with the Sheffield/Worksop line, though the following photos do not appear in the order in which they were taken. This station closed in 1964, but has since re-opened. The previous Nottingham/Worksop service was so slow south of here due to mining subsidence that I became bored with the train journey. *5108*

Near Nether Langwith, Notts; Class 45s, 13.05 St Pancras-Sheffield (left) and equivalent 15.00 from Sheffield, 31 March 1975.
The parallel (on the left) LD&ECR has been closed hereabouts and a new spur to the Midland constructed north of Shirebrook. My 'Talking of Trains' trip in the Eastern GM saloon on 3 May 1975 was almost certainly the first train over the curve with fare-paying passengers. *5114*

Shirebrook Junction, Notts, Class 45, 15.47 Sheffield-St Pancras, 31 March 1975.
This picture is out of geographical sequence, as it warrants a whole page reproduction. At that date the tracks to the right still went through Ollerton to Lincoln (Pyewipe Junction), but normally carried only freight and holiday specials. 5109

Above Whitwell Tunnel, Notts; Class 45, 09.50 Edinburgh-Penzance, 31 March 1975.
I have trespassed, which is very unusual for me, but I had to capture the rare sight of this working emerging from the south portal of the tunnel. I wonder how often the train came this way? It is helpful that the destination indicator points to the Western Region. *5125*

Below Whitwell, Notts; Class 45, 14.05 St Pancras-Sheffield, 31 March 1975.
Bearing the number 1E41, this is clearly heading from the London Midland to the Eastern Region of BR, crossing the imaginary boundary at Clay Cross. The northern portal of the tunnel is visible behind the train and adjacent bridge. *5127*

Whitwell, Notts; Class 45, Penzance-Edinburgh, 31 March 1975.
I think this must be the train indicated, though the 1M32 puzzles me as in theory there should be an 'S' in the blind. Whitwell station closed in 1964 but remained in good condition until replaced by the more modern structure when passenger trains restarted. *5130*

Above Woodend Junction, Notts; Class 45, 11.00 Sheffield-St Pancras, 31 March 1975.
I hesitated to climb the steps to this location, but happily the signalman called out to me to come up and join him, which I gladly did! We are at the southern tip of a triangle from the Sheffield/Worksop line and the express is rounding the western spur. *5134*

Below Shireoaks West Junction, Notts; Class 45, 09.16 Leeds-St Pancras, 31 March 1975.
This was my first photo of the day as I returned south after spending Easter at Nawton in my new house (of six months), which I then used as a holiday cottage. The loops precede Shireoaks station from the east; it is the boundary with the London Midland Region of BR. *4349*

Barnby Moor & Sutton, Notts; Class 47, 15.25 Leeds-King's Cross, 30 September 1976.
We've now left the Midland diversions for the East Coast Main Line. The last trains called at this station on 7 November 1949, and the adjoining level crossing of the former Great North Road was replaced long ago by a bridge – today the service on the East Coast Main Line hardly acknowledges its existence. In the far distance is Ranskill, where the signalman used to give warning of northbound delays at Doncaster. The box there still survives by a lifting barrier and a strip of public land along the line. 5435

Hexthorpe Junction, South Yorks; DMU, 11.30 Sheffield-Hull, 20 June 1975.
I've yet to reach Dearn Valley Coaches! This point marks the southern end of the line from Bentley Junction (towards Hull), which avoids Doncaster station. One of the few trains – only freight – to come this way is the 09.50 Lindsey-Rectory Junction oil tanks on Tuesdays and Thursdays only. I expected to see it cross the Don Viaduct on 8 December 2005 with Neal Pursglove, but it ran 15 minutes earlier than expected so I will have to go again. I'm glad that I heard it in the cutting as we arrived; at least that avoided a pointless long wait in the cold. When we traversed the line in the saloon the driver had to obtain a paper indicating that the normal signalling applied to us – otherwise freight trains were allowed to proceed one behind the other when traffic was heavy. Behind the DMU is a very deep cutting. 5453

Wombersley, North Yorks; Class 47, down 'merry-go-round' (MGR) coal train (6K90), 28 March 1975.
I'm on my way to Nawton and reconnoitring the route of the GM saloon, which we are to charter on 3 May. It so happened that when we reached here in the train (southbound) the signal was at danger and our Inspector had to visit the box to ascertain the cause – the next box was unmanned! We had to proceed at caution and I was advised not to charter a train again on Cup Final Day! 5489

Adwick-le-Street, South Yorks; Class 47, 11.30 Leeds-King's Cross, 20 June 1975.
This station is now the terminus of some trains from Sheffield that provide an excellent 'Park & Ride' service with competitive fares to Doncaster. They reverse on the spur to Skellow on the freight line to Stainforth & Hatfield. I parked here when photographing at Doncaster the last few Eurostar trains on the Leeds service. 5473

Above Heck, North Yorks; Class 55 'Deltic', 10.30 Newcastle-King's Cross, 17 May 1979.

I'm driving to Nawton with Gavin. Little did we realise that years later this was to be the location where a vehicle left the M62 and was hit by an up express, which then lay in the path of a down freight – quite dreadful and totally inexcusable. The media questioned why the freight train should have come along just then, rather than why a car should be on the line. The drip-drip propaganda of such as the British Road Federation is having its media effect, and privatisation does not seem to have improved the image. While the train is bound to follow its track, those undisciplined folk who get in its way receive undue sympathy – no reporter seems to consider the feelings of the engine driver. From the train I cannot see any new protective fencing on the M62, though the County Engineer has been busy improving road/rail protection in North Yorkshire, and not just on main roads. According to 'Freightmaster', cement/concrete traffic originates here from Plasmor and goes to the Thames estuary at Bow. *5494*

Below Selby, North Yorks; Class 47 No 47416, 13.00 King's Cross-Edinburgh, 28 March 1975.

What a bonus the Selby coalfield proved to be with the construction of a loop line avoiding this swing bridge with its severe speed restrictions and tortuous curves, not to mention the occasions when boats had to be given priority! But how short was the life of the coalfield as compared with the railway… *5508*

York, North Yorks; Class 45, 10.12 Newcastle-Cardiff, 13 May 1976.
I was awaiting the London train when this service arrived and increased the interest. Presumably I had lunch in the dining-car as my diary records 'four waitresses' – the service must have been good! The environment at York station is marvellous, though it is wise to wrap up against the wind-tunnel effect on cold days. 6898

Thirsk, North Yorks; HST No 253020, up trial run as empty stock, 22 April 1977.
As you can tell from the lighting, it is quite late in the day. In fact, earlier I had been giving a session at the late-lamented Woking Staff College for professional transport folk on their way to the top. It was always a joy and a stimulus to go there. I used to represent local government (a Minister used to come from central government!), give a 30-minute lecture and a similar time for slides and questions. And what penetrating questions they were! I used to enjoy playing the railwaymen against the bus men and the occasional enterprising road haulier, and vice versa. One of my favourite problems was illustrated in Kirkbymoorside where a brewer's dray was unloading opposite a parked car with the result that the bus could not get through. Who should have priority? Naturally the answer invariably was the brewer's dray, and few thought about the passengers, probably old and infirm, waiting in the rain all the way to Scarborough because the bus had been delayed. *7051*

Above Bradbury Carrs, Co Durham; Class 45, 08.10 Liverpool (Lime Street)-Newcastle Central, 28 August 1975.
There is an element of doubt about the exact date. Having climbed in a series of curves out of Darlington, the line then straightens out across the levels towards Ferryhill and Durham. 7566

Below Slaggyford, Northumberland; DMU, Alston-Haltwhistle, date uncertain.
In the days before 1974, of the Rural District Councils' Association the smallest authority was Alston with Carrigill. The leader of the council owned a local factory and made a point of sending his products by rail. Eventually he was told that they could not be accepted on the train, and in due course (after the construction of an expensive road bridge near Coanwood) the line duly closed. 7698

Above Scremerston, Northumberland; Class 47 No 47420, 10.40 Edinburgh-King's Cross, 27 August 1977.
I had travelled to Berwick on Tweed by train the previous day, but although three staff were in evidence, including the steward, no dinner was forthcoming. Perhaps the chef hadn't turned up. This is the point at which the train really gets near the sea, and the view can be enchanting. Note milepost 64, presumably from Newcastle. 8067

Below Spittal, Northumberland; Class 47, 11.25 Edinburgh-King's Cross, 27 August 1977.
We really are close to the sea now, though we have still to reach Berwick from the south. This little track wanders down to the beach. My next pictures of the East Coast Main Line are found in the chapter on Scotland. 8076

Knaresborough, North Yorks; DMU, 10.50 York-Leeds, 10 May 1976.
This is a notable viaduct and tourist attraction. Usually trains run at 30-minute intervals between here and Leeds, and continue to York each hour. The line was threatened with closure in the Beeching era but retained as a condition of the merger of the Eastern and North Eastern Regions of BR. There is no equivalent bus service between here and York and the trains load well most of the time. Operationally it is a time-warp, and none the worse for that. 6948

Above Kirk Hammerton, North Yorks; DMU, 10.51 Leeds-York, 24 April 1976.

It's my birthday and I've come to photograph *Hardwick* and the Midland Compound on a special train. Double track is retained between Hammerton and Cattal so that the hourly trains can pass each other on an otherwise single line. I wonder how many liveries these DMUs carried? 6933

Below Copmanthorpe, North Yorks; Class 47, NRM catering special (10.50 York-King's Cross), 13 September 1979.

Having stayed at Barnby Moor overnight, I am on my way to a conference due to start at 11 o'clock in York but decide to arrive a few minutes late so as to witness the departure of this unusual train to mark the centenary of railway catering. I wonder whether such an innovation would be possible today? 4545

Above Ulleskelf, North Yorks; Class 31, down ballast train (6F41), date uncertain.

This is one of those awkward stations. It's obvious that the twice-daily train to and from Sheffield should call as it is sited on the tracks they use – but you can go from here to Hull or Scarborough at times and come from Beverley and Blackpool. Clearly some workings cross from the Leeds lines at Church Fenton. I recall that years ago a Newquay holiday train stopped here to pick up! The bus is an archive in itself. *4557*

Below Church Fenton, North Yorks; DMU, 15.15 York-Liverpool (Lime Street), 17 May 1979.

If this picture was reproduced in colour you would see the tangerine-painted signs of the former North Eastern Region of BR. Note also the long slope to the platforms, with their covered awnings. On the far side of the left-hand platform I once joined the 7.44am to Leeds via Tadcaster (having come from London by sleeper to Leeds overnight). There was no return working, so we had the DMU to ourselves as far as Wetherby. The passenger service came to an end in 1964; had a circular working been retained, there might be less congestion on the streets of Leeds today. *4561*

Above South Milford, North Yorks; Class 47 No 47299, southbound freight (6M60), 17 May 1979.
This is the original route from London (Euston) via Derby and Leicester, the first to enter York from the south with regular trains from 9 November 1840. Today there are normally only two workings to and from Sheffield, and a Virgin express each way, but there is plenty of freight. The line running across the back of the picture is the Leeds & Selby, over which in the early days the promoter George Hudson discontinued the trains so as to divert them via Castleford at higher fares. The connecting curve appears in the picture below. *4571*

Below Milford Curve from Gascoigne Wood, North Yorks; Class 47 No 47371, MGR coal train (6K89), 17 May 1979.
I wonder whether the 'K' in the destination refers to Knottingley? At Burton Salmon Junction the lines part for Pontefract and Castleford respectively. On a professional visit from the office to Selby District Council to discuss some policy matter, I was faced by row upon row of miners. Clearly they were not favourably impressed by this snooty Londoner! Although my subject was entirely local government orientated, they decided to test me before I began and I was asked why at Burton Salmon the Knottingley line had a speed restriction whereas the line to Castleford did not. (Someone must have known of my railway hobby.) I thought for a moment, then said that the restricted line must be affected by mining subsidence. A round of spontaneous applause followed – they would then have believed anything I said! *4572*

Brotherton, North Yorks; Class 47s, Penzance-Edinburgh and Edinburgh-Penzance, 17 May 1979.
I'm looking across Fairburn Ings into South Yorkshire. This train has been re-routed several times: I recall when it went via Pontefract, then via Castleford, and now via Leeds or Doncaster. This route is allocated to freight.

The second picture shows the southbound train: in my experience the up and down trains have always passed in this vicinity. *4588/4589*

Above Micklefield, North Yorks; Class 45, 10.05 Liverpool (Lime Street)-Newcastle Central, date unknown.
This site has changed out of all recognition. The mine has gone, the track has been rationalised, the signal box (Peckfield) has been replaced and the signals worked from afar, and for years the land has been offered for redevelopment, which has not happened. The snow has gone too. I used to enjoy travelling on these trains from Thirsk to Manchester for meetings there in my retirement. The 1st Class fare was refunded and I used to sit in my compartment like Lord Tom Noddy enjoying every moment! 6349

Below Ingber, North Yorks; Class 40 No 40005, down coal train, 21 June 1975.
A series of illustrations of the Settle & Carlisle and associated lines now follows. This train has just passed above the Leeds & Liverpool Canal as it crosses an aqueduct over the River Aire. 8411

Ingber, North Yorks; Class 45, 10.45 Glasgow (Central)-St Pancras 'Thames-Clyde Express', 21 June 1975.
This train's name was dropped during 1975 when it ceased to run from and to London. *8412*

Hellifield, North Yorks; Class 50, up freight (6V57), 21 June 1975.
This is a station with listed status and its condition deteriorated very seriously for many years. Now it has been put right and is a joy to behold with its bright ironwork and Midland Railway insignia. When the S&C was under threat of closure, one proposal was for a steam shed here and excursions northbound. A new road has been put in from the A65 to aid development. The Royal Train stood here for some time in 2005 with *Duchess of Sutherland* before Prince Charles joined the footplate at Kirkby Stephen for a trip to Appleby. *8427*

Above **Clapham, North Yorks; DMU, 10.03 Morecambe-Leeds, 21 June 1975.**
Today the train cannot be seen from this location due to the growth of trees and shrubs, which have hidden the line in a virtual cutting. Until 1964 this was the junction for Ingleton and the West Coast Main Line at Low Gill. 8555

Below **Runley Bridge, North Yorks; Class 45, 09.35 Carlisle-Nottingham (Midland), 21 May 1977.**
We're still south of Settle, but Pen-y-Ghent is on the northern horizon marking our entry into Ribblesdale, and shortly we shall encounter the fells. 8640

Above Langcliffe Mill, North Yorks; Class 45, up 'Thames Clyde Express' (1A86), 21 June 1975.
The fells are now even nearer. I'm on a footbridge that unites a pleasant circular walk from Settle out along the river and back through the villages. 8683

Below Helwith Bridge, North Yorks; Class 45, centenary special, St Pancras-Carlisle, 1 May 1976.
Sadly it proved to be a day of incessant pouring rain, but despite that it ended with a banquet in a marquee in the station yard at Settle, though we had to put our feet on duckboards to prevent them getting wet. Bishop Eric Treacy gave an address as though nothing untoward was happening, and the dinner was piping hot, much to my surprise in the circumstances. Earlier *Flying Scotsman* and *Hardwick* had hauled another special, which I photographed at Bentham, including vintage coaches from the NRM. The Keeper, the late Dr Coiley, spent much of the day on board bailing out water with buckets from the leaking roofs; he was glad of a rest when it reached Hellifield! 8699

Above Helwith Bridge, North Yorks; Class 25 No 25279, ballast train from Ribblehead, 1 May 1976.

A quarry road from here leads to a parking place from which one can walk adjacent to the line, with Pen-y-Ghent dominating the eastern skyline. *8704*

Below Ribblehead, North Yorks; Class 45, 10.20 Nottingham (Midland)-Glasgow (Central), 18 September 1976.

What a miserable day, but what a view! *8787*

Above Blea Moor, North Yorks; Class 45, 10.45 Glasgow
(Central)-Nottingham (Midland), 18 September 1976.
Although BR denied intentions to close the S&C, we now know (*The
Battle for the Settle & Carlisle* by James Towler, Chairman of the local
TUCC, Platform 5 Publishing Ltd, 1990) that the curtailment of trains
at Nottingham was a precursor, and soon they were to be diverted via
Shap as Ribblehead Viaduct was said to be falling down. Fortunately
the strength of public opinion and Lord Whitelaw, whose constituency
just included the line, persuaded Lady Thatcher not to authorise
closure and the future of this major tourist attraction looks bright.
Unless piped water has now been connected to Blea Moor box (and

Network Rail has done many signal boxes proud) the DMU from Leeds
brings a supply when it terminates at Ribblehead and runs forward to
assist. *8792*

Below Dent Head Viaduct, North Yorks; Class 45, up freight,
29 April 1976.
At the rear of the train there used to be a signal box connected south
to Blea Moor and north to Dent – today the section is Blea Moor to
Garsdale. From the hillside above the train there is a superb view of the
viaduct and the mouth of Blea Moor Tunnel – a really striking piece of
railway construction. *8837*

Above Arten Gill Viaduct, North Yorks; Class 45, 08.00
St Pancras-Glasgow (Central), 21 June 1975.
This is the next viaduct to the north and really makes an artistic
setting. There is a track on the south side and it is possible to pass
beneath and climb above the far side. I'm standing near a cottage that
sometimes sells teas and coffee. 8879

Below Crosby Garrett Viaduct, Cumbria; Class 47, 07.15
Nottingham (Midland)-Glasgow (Central), 30 September 1978.
Although the weather is inclement it cannot entirely spoil this view
from the old station (closed 1952 and not re-opened) with the tunnel
in the distance. Below and hidden from view is the charming village
street with a stream down the middle, spoiled only by a road haulage
depot by the railway. 8993

Garsdale, Cumbria; Class 25s, up cement train, 18 September 1976.

I'm taking this picture from the so-called 'coal road', which comes over the top from Dent station. The railway went north and entered Rise Hill Tunnel, but since emerging it has hugged the south side of Garsdale; however, as you can see it is about to resume its northward trend. The road from Wensleydale to Sedbergh passes under the line at The Gamecock. 8952

Levens Viaduct, Cumbria; Class 47, 11.15 Euston-Barrow in Furness, 24 May 1975.
I had to have a new battery fixed in my car this morning. It had failed at Shap the previous evening, but fortunately I was facing downhill and could start and keep going to my digs in Windermere. There are a lot of streams below me; I was wandering among them trying to find my way out when a man on the high ground called down and guided me through. There are no longer London trains here (or sleepers), Manchester Airport being a frequent destination. Ulverston lies across the water. *9488*

Plumpton Junction, Cumbria; DMU, 11.00 Preston-Barrow, 21 June 1975.
At this point freight trains took on bankers through Ulverston to Lindal. It was also the junction for Lakeside and for Conishead Priory (or later Glaxo Chemicals), but the box has now been taken out of use. *9507*

4.
THE EAST

East Anglia was one of the first regions to receive diesel multiple units in the 1950s – and it certainly deserved them. When undertaking my National Service (1951-53) at Honington on the Norfolk/Suffolk border, I travelled to and from Liverpool Street at the weekend. I recall leaving Bury St Edmunds on Saturday at 1.30pm and not reaching the City until 4.50pm, with 15 minutes between trains at Ipswich – nearly 3½ hours for about 95 miles, and almost invariably late. The engines and stock were worn out. Sometimes we would be able to catch the 12.23pm from Bury, but BR retimed this to 12.15 so we couldn't make it. I determined to outwit them and chartered a string of taxis to the next station east, Thurston. We could then just do it, and did! Eventually a ticket collector had to be sent there. When closure proposals were mooted it was realised that the Minister of Transport at the time lived nearby. As a result it is still open, well maintained and houses suitable offices.

When the 'Britannia' Class steam engines were introduced, Norwich came within 2 hours of London (115 miles), and electrification has improved on this a little. Indeed, Ipswich can be reached now in just under the hour. At the same time freight continues to grow from Felixstowe and the resultant track improvements are in evidence as far as Ely and beyond.

It seems a pity, therefore, that in 1959 we had to lose the Midland & Great Northern network, as the A17, which follows its trunk route, is lorry-laden every time I drive that way. The East Lincs line was banished in 1970, and the GC between Gainsborough and Barnetby sees passenger trains only on Saturdays. How closure could be applied to a service linking Norwich, Wymondham, Dereham, Swaffham and King's Lynn beggars belief (like York-Pocklington-Market Weighton-Beverley-Hull), and shows every sign of short-term thinking. On the one hand there was F. C. Margetts seeking to close down lines from his office in York, and on the other hand Gerard Fiennes, the Eastern Region General Manager, on the ground seeking to improve them with due economy – the railwayman-cum-pseudo-politician against the true railwayman. When the Chairman of BR, Stanley Raymond, dismissed Fiennes for publishing an autobiographical critique of railway management, the sequel was his dismissal by the Minister of Transport. 'In my twenty-one years in public transport,' Raymond recalled, 'I calculate that at least half my time has been devoted to organisation, reorganisation, acquisition, denationalisation, centralisation, decentralisation, according to the requirements of the now regular political quinquennial revaluation of national transport policy.' Perhaps that was really the essence of the job; little attempt was made to get the public on side. Now that we know how readily the Treasury cut finance to BR, it speaks well for them that they were able to effect as many improvements to the main line services as they did. We have not seen the like since that time. Where has the money gone instead?

Above right Great Hickle Farm, Essex; Class 47, 09.54 Yarmouth-Liverpool Street, 27 March 1976.
I'm on the main line from London to Norwich before it was electrified on the overhead system, at an overbridge between Colchester and Manningtree not far from Dedham. *5648*

Right Mistley, Essex; Class 31, 12.52 Harwich-Peterborough, 27 March 1976.
This was a working of long standing that used the north-to-east spur at Manningtree to gain Ipswich and East Anglia. Like the famous Harwich/Manchester (formerly Liverpool) boat train via Lincoln and the Woodhead route, it has passed into history. The siding served a grain terminal. *5652*

Brundell, Norfolk; Class 31, Yarmouth-Birmingham, 6 August 1977.
This is the junction of the two routes from Yarmouth (via Acle or Reedham) and from Lowestoft. The DMU on the left is probably awaiting access to the single line ahead. 5775

Above Reedham, Norfolk; Class 47, 14.30 Yarmouth-Derby,
6 August 1977.
By the bridge you can see the signals for the main line to Lowestoft and
(left) the single track to Yarmouth from which this train has come via
that extraordinary halt at Berney Arms. *5766*

Below Reedham Junction, Norfolk; Class 37 No 37075,
Yarmouth-Newcastle, 6 August 1977.
Here you can see a train winding through the junction with the
Lowestoft lines. Traffic increased significantly in this area in those days
with holiday trains each Saturday in the summer. They avoided the
terminus at Norwich by using the Trowse curve, which has since been
lifted. *5763*

Above left Cromer, Norfolk; DMU, 10.30 Sheringham-Norwich, 21 February 1975.
The track layout can be misleading as it represents two branch lines, the left-hand from Sheringham and the other from Norwich via North Walsham. The one station that survives at Cromer is very neat, with its adjacent supermarket built on the goods yard. *5810*

Left Spalding, Lincs; Class 47, up freight, date uncertain.
This station has suffered a considerable reduction in traffic. Until 1970 it was on the main line from London to Grimsby, with dining-car trains at appropriate times of day; then these were diverted via Newark and subsequently disappeared altogether. The Harwich-Manchester boat train called here, but the line it followed from March was closed in 1982. The Midland & Great Northern route trains from Birmingham/ Nottingham to King's Lynn/Yarmouth were withdrawn in 1959. The surviving service from Peterborough was re-introduced only at the instigation of the local authorities. Today passenger trains ply between Peterborough, Sleaford, Lincoln and Doncaster, but the station, with just two platforms, looks quite neat and clean. In the late afternoon the 11.54 Felixstowe-Healey Mills paper train has run this way to avoid the East Coast Main Line, but is not shown in the latest edition of 'Freightmaster'. *5974*

Above Littleport, Cambs; Class 37, 17.24 King's Lynn-Liverpool Street, 27 March 1976.
Keen observers of my text will notice that my journey has described an arc from the Harwich branch to this line, and I am enjoying yet another 'Talking of Trains' coach tour. This line has since been modernised with overhead electrification and most trains terminate in London at King's Cross (via Hitchin) rather than Liverpool Street, which was the traditional pattern. There is a freight train of sand from Middleton Towers via King's Lynn to either Barnby Dun or Monk Bretton, depending on the day of the week. *5898*

Above Near Clifton on Trent, Notts; Class 47, down coal (8P89),
27 March 1975.
This is quite a rare view here, showing a train east of the Trent on the
former Lancashire, Derbyshire & East Coast Railway heading for
Pyewipe Junction, Lincoln, in the late afternoon. You can see High
Marnham Power Station in the distance. As already stated on page 54,
this is now mothballed. The line on which the train is running closed
in 1980. *4320*

Below Clarborough Tunnel, Notts; DMU, 09.27 Sheffield
(Midland)-Lincoln Central, **27 March 1975.**
I have walked some distance across the fields from the nearest road to
gain this foot crossing. Was it worth it? I think so to complete the set
of pictures hereby. *6189*

Above **Stallingborough, Lincs; DMU, 09.45 Manchester (Piccadilly)-Cleethorpes, October 1975.**
At Barnetby one tends to think that Grimsby and Cleethorpes are just around the corner, but not so. There are several intermediate stations, none of which have closed, so long-distance services have to make calls at quite remote rural places. *6319*

Below **Healing, Lincs; Class 47, 12.53 Cleethorpes-King's Cross, October 1975.**
Here we are at the next station east. The train in the picture replaced the direct East Lincolnshire Line service to Peterborough and itself has since been withdrawn. *6321*

Thorne North, South Yorks; 'Trans-Pennine' DMU, 09.45 Manchester (Piccadilly)-Hull, 17 May 1979.
We are north of the Humber estuary now, and the Trans-Pennine unit is travelling eastbound. The junction for Grimsby is round the corner behind the train, hence Thorne has two stations, North and South.

The Railway Enthusiasts Club of Farnborough in Hampshire once (21 April 1963) operated Fountain Coaches of Twickenham between the stations in connection with a special they chartered. Unusually I include two pictures of the same train, but the view is worth it! *5455/5456*

Goole, Humberside; DMU, 12.40 Sheffield (Midland)-Hull, 22 August 1976.
It was anticipated that this would become the terminus from the west and that the swing bridge over the River Ouse could be laid to rest. I had the privilege of videoing this when I first retired and was amazed that the machinery that turned the structure still bore the date 1868 – it really was vintage. However, the NUR had other ideas and raised such opposition that the through service continues to this day, though expresses run via Selby. The next few pictures follow the line to Hull. 5459

Saltmarshe, Humberside; Class 31, 09.10 King's Cross-Hull (and Leeds from Doncaster), 27 March 1975.
I'm now east of the Goole swing bridge, which is rivalled by a lofty structure on the M62. This is a remote place but the peak-hour service is still quite acceptable. 5463

Above Gilberdyke, Humberside; Class 20, officers' special (5G01), 27 March 1975.
I wonder if they are having a drink on board? Since this picture was taken the layout has been reduced to two tracks. The junction for Goole/Selby is behind me; the signal box used to be called Staddlethorpe. *6360*

Below Ferriby, Humberside; Class 55 'Deltic', westbound light engine, 22 September 1979.
We're having a day out in the Eastern Region GM's Saloon and arranged to stop here for photographs for about 10 minutes before heading for Scarborough. Unexpectedly this loco appeared and must have been much recorded from the footbridge. *6374*

Above Hessle, Humberside; Class 47, 12.45 King's Cross-Hull (1D03), 27 March 1975.

Today the Humber road bridge stands high above the back of the view, a wonder of engineering and a valuable asset for me to drive into north Lincolnshire and beyond. At one time it was thought that the M11 might be extended here from Cambridge, but that idea seems to be in long abeyance. 6375

Below Burton Lane Junction, York; DMU, empty stock to Rowntrees Halt, 24 June 1977.

The unit is ready for the evening departure (sometimes Doncaster, sometimes Sheffield). By this junction trains ran to Foss Islands yard and ventured on to the Derwent Valley Railway (to Cliff Common near Selby), which I used on an RCTS Special to Newcastle via Tadcaster, Arthington north curve, Carlisle and Alston! It was said always to be in profit, but closed throughout in 1972. 6472

Kirkham Priory, North Yorks; Class 40, 13.24 Newcastle-Scarborough, 3 July 1976.
I've just seen *Flying Scotsman* pass, on a special. This train is the one survivor of those that used to avoid the reversal in York by going through Gilling and doing a shunt at Malton. The whole area – the river, the ruins and general setting – is charming. 6546

Kirkham Abbey, North Yorks; Class 31 No 31251 and brake-van, 25 May 1979. The signal box and, I believe, even the level crossing gates are listed, so cannot easily be removed. The old station, which closed in 1930, lost its tea-room a year or two back. 6545

Heslerton, North Yorks; Class 37, 09.22 Birmingham (New Street)-Scarborough, 3 July 1976.
The wayside stations along here were closed as long ago as 1930. The signal box survived for at least another 50 years but has now gone too, the section being Malton-Weaverthorpe. 6608

Above **Heslerton, North Yorks; DMU, 12.13 Scarborough-Liverpool (Lime Street), 3 July 1976.**
Here is the signal box mentioned on the previous page. *6612*

Below **Flamborough, Humberside; Class 47, 11.12 King's Cross-Scarborough, 9 July 1977.**
We have already seen this working at the start of the book. When opened the station was called Marton; it closed in 1970. There used to be double track here. *6422*

Filey, North Yorks; DMU, 09.53 Hull-Scarborough, 11 May 1976.
The first train of the weekday runs here as empty stock, then forms a service to York via Scarborough and on to Manchester Airport.
The overall roof has been cleaned up and repaired in recent years. 6466

Battersby, North Yorks; DMUs, 16.11 from Whitby (left) and 16.40 from Middlesbrough, 3 July 1976.
Since the withdrawal of the passenger service west to Picton in 1954, the Esk Valley trains have reversed here before proceeding to Teesside. It is likely to become a Community Railway – only the inability of coaches regularly to mount Limber Hill and the need for school trains have saved the branch. Its future could be bright with tourists, but the North Yorkshire Moors Railway (from Pickering to Grosmont) has not yet been allowed to run its steam trains west of Glaisdale, even though the timetable provides time for it. One of the railway's locos, 'K1' No 2005, can be seen on the left of the picture. 6861

5.
SCOTLAND

All the Highland lines feature in this period from 1975 to 1979. Because we are limited to certain years I feared that the output might be restricted, but apart from the Nith Valley and the line to Stranraer we seem to travel widely. I did not picture the West Coast Main Line to any extent until quite recent years.

The electrification of the East Coast Main Line must be one of the major achievements since that time, though I was intrigued that Eurostar sets could not operate north of York because of traction problems and that the fairly frequent collapse of the overhead wires always seems to occur on four-track sections. The increase in frequency of service on this route is also worthy of comment. Indeed, GNER and Virgin trains seem to compete with each other for space – privatisation in practice, perhaps. However, Dunbar has lost out for direct London runs.

One named service that disappeared without ceremony was 'The Clansman', a weekday train from Inverness to Euston via Birmingham and vice versa; it is illustrated here. London is gained from the Highlands only by day via the East Coast; the sleepers, however, still travel West Coast, and Fort William has managed to retain its one through service.

The Scottish Assembly has to show its mettle, and some small innovations have occurred. Will Edinburgh-Hawick follow? It is important to see that transport public expenditure is fairly distributed between rail and road. The restoration of passenger trains along the Firth of Forth towards Stirling seems to be happening.

As regards electrification, it is interesting to read the White Paper 'Proposals for the Railways' of October 1956, which promised to give diesels a 'thorough and selective trial'. Six months later it was said officially that 'the ultimate object was electrification of all main lines... By the end of the century the need for a big fleet of diesel locomotives would have disappeared.' How wrong was this thesis! I sometimes wonder what proportion of trains on electrified lines take current – it is rare to see a freight train so hauled.

The loss of Motorail between England and Scotland is disappointing. The argument went that motorists would take to the motorways and leave the trains empty. And so they might, but not for long. Who enjoys motorway driving? Not only did the train provide a sleeper and dinner beforehand, but two days were gained for a holiday. I still hope such trains may return – and from York as well as London!

Above right Lamberton, Borders; Class 47, 08.15 Doncaster-Edinburgh (Waverley), 27 August 1977.
I've joined John Wylde and his family who have lived in a number of locations in this area and we are exploring viewpoints along the East Coast Main Line. It makes a change to be directed by someone else. I was interested to observe in the Jeremy Paxman episode of the BBC's *Who Do You Think You Are?* family roots series early in 2006 that the TV camera caught the distinct view of the streets of Tweedmouth as his train climbed on to the Royal Border Bridge. *8106*

Right Horn Burn, near Ayton, Borders; Class 37, 08.03 Glasgow-Scarborough via York, 26 August 1978.
This is a favourite location for me. My custom is to witness the 4pm from Edinburgh, which used to be followed closely (sometimes on yellow aspects) by the mail from Glasgow to Newcastle, quite often an EMU in recent years. The field to the left allows a wider view of the landscape than shown here. *8135*

Horn Burn, near Ayton, Borders; Class 45, 09.40 Edinburgh-Plymouth (*above*) and Class 40, relief to Plymouth train, 26 August 1978.
Soon after breakfast (at Ayton on this occasion) I ventured out to this field to watch a procession of holiday trains come south. *8136/8138*

Restonhill, Borders; Class 55 'Deltic', up 'Flying Scotsman' 10.10 Edinburgh-King's Cross, 26 August 1978.
Reston (station closed 1964) used to be a major cattle market and was the junction for Duns (until 1951, goods 1966) and Greenlaw in 1948). In latter years the branch was steam-worked from Tweedmouth, but on English Bank Holidays the goods continued to run, albeit hauled by a diesel from Edinburgh. *8141*

Cockburnspath, Borders; Class 45, 15.00 Edinburgh (Waverley)-Newcastle Central local, 27 August 1977.
This is the summit of the line and southbound it leaves the coast to go inland. Stopping services were rare, and there weren't many stations at which to call. Just round the corner behind the train is a magnificent arch over the Dunglass Burn. *8180*

Above North of Grantshouse, Borders; Class 55 'Deltic, 13.00 King's Cross-Edinburgh (Waverley), 27 August 1977.
The summer evening is assisting photography. The building by the A1 used to be a café with a good reputation, but it was closed when I passed by last year. In the colour section (page VII) is the view north from this spot. It took a long walk to get here. *8172*

Below Broomhills, near Beattock, Dumfries & Galloway; DMUs running empty from Glasgow area to Norwich and/or Neville Hill on transfer; 16 May 1975.
I'm on the West Coast Main Line now and this train is a surprise. The detail is supplied by John Edgington. *10031*

Above Ardock, Strathclyde; Class 45, Glasgow (Central)-Carlisle, 15 May 1975.
This is the working that was out and back to Leeds in a day – good utilisation of rolling-stock! It followed the Settle & Carlisle route. 9983

Below Ballochmyle, Strathclyde; DMU, 17.30 Glasgow (Central)-Carlisle, 15 May 1975.
Just behind the train is the Ballochmyle Viaduct, which is now the highest railway bridge in Great Britain. The masonry arch has a semi-circular span of 181 feet and carries the line 169 feet above the River Ayr. It was built between 1846 and 1848. *10003*

Above Near Lugton, Strathclyde; Class 45, 16.10 Glasgow (Central)-Leeds (1E31), 15 May 1975.

When it was deemed necessary to rationalise certain lines, the double track was removed from the Glasgow & South Western route here between Barrhead and Kilmarnock, and again between Annan and Gretna. Now that freight traffic has developed, particularly coal to the south, there is talk of restoring the section along the Solway. *10009*

Below Lochwinnoch, Strathclyde; DMU, 15.00 Glasgow (Central)-Ayr, 15 May 1975.

The route of this service has been electrified overhead and the signals have been replaced by colour lights. You can tell that my itinerary encompasses several locations in this area. In the morning I brought the car on the boat from Brodick on Arran to Ardrossan. *9930*

Above Orton, Grampian; DMU, 12.42 Inverness-Aberdeen,
25 October 1978.
I've gone north to near the Moray Firth for this picture and am
intrigued that the DMU has an extra unit at the back, presumably to
quicken it up – rather like between Crewe and Cardiff at one time. In
1980 I was to include a stop at the next station north – Orbliston
(closed 1964), junction for Fochabers Town, and home of Baxter's soup
– much to the surprise of the residents of the station house. We had the
two Scottish saloons, diesel-hauled, and photographed ourselves in the
sunshine among the blooming gorse! *10780*

Below Whitefield Croft, Grampian; Class 47, Burghead-
Doncaster malt train, 25 October 1978.
The 'water of life' in vats! The branch joined the Forres-Elgin line at
Alves. Our saloons had gone down there and were propelled at high
speed northbound while we sat in the front! Presumably someone was
look-out. *10789*

Above Alves, Grampian; DMU, 10.40 Inverness-Aberdeen, 25 October 1978.

And here we are at Alves station, closed in 1965. The junction for Burghead (closed to passengers in 1931) is at the back of the picture. I have subsequently obtained pictures there with the branch train waiting for the road to Elgin, but the bridge seems constantly under repair so as to be awkward of access. *10792*

Below Milton of Grange, Grampian; Class 26, Elgin-Inverness freight, 25 October 1978.

Because this train shunts at Forres we were able to take pictures of it before and after that town – was it worth it? Yes, because little freight runs this way. *10799*

Forres, Grampian; DMU, 14.42 Inverness-Aberdeen, 25 October 1978.
The platform is on a curve, a legacy of the days when trains turned south here (pre-1965) from Inverness to Aviemore and Euston and there was a triangle of tracks. *10805*

Newton of Dalvey, Grampian; Class 26, Elgin-Inverness freight, 25 October 1978.
Here we are west of Forres and the train is entering more undulating country. *10809*

Nairn, Grampian; DMU, 13.50 Aberdeen-Inverness, 25 October 1978.
This is the last photo in our series along the Moray Firth. The platform at Nairn and the location of two signal boxes meant that the staff were provided with a cycle to get quickly between the two. It is a fine town and well worth a visit. The late Cyril Walmesley and I were based at Grantown-on-Spey at the time, having come north by Motorail. *10814*

Pitlochry, Tayside; Class 47, Inverness-Crewe Motorail, 31 August 1979.
This train ran on Fridays only and there seemed to be no equivalent northbound; I have mislaid my Motorail brochures so cannot amplify further at present. The Chief Passenger Manager at York, the late 'Uncle' Bert Gemmell, had kindly provided Gavin and myself with two 1st Class tickets from London to Wick and Thurso. Therefore the previous night we came up to Perth on the 22.35 sleeper from Euston. I recall that we said goodnight to each other out of the windows of the adjacent sleepers while the post was loaded at Bletchley – sounds rather sloppy now! After breakfast in the Station Hotel we moved on to Pitlochry in order to take this picture, and subsequently stayed the next night in Inverness. *10839*

Left Killiecrankie, Tayside; Class 47, 10.35 Inverness-Euston via Birmingham, 'The Clansman', 23 October 1978.
On the cover of this book is a train about to enter the southern portal of the tunnel here. This one is facing the north end. I wonder why Euston lost out to King's Cross for the London train? It was discontinued in 1992. *10846*

Below Aldclune, Tayside; Class 26, mixed freight to Inverness, 21 May 1985.
Obviously this picture should not be here because of its date, but, having made a mistake, I thought we would leave it, perhaps as a foretaste of books to come? The A9 looks quiet because it has been realigned over the bridge on which we are standing. Trevor Owen and I are waiting for the first 'Royal Scotsman' to come from Boat of Garten to Edinburgh and this train just happened to appear. *10847*

Right Near Blair Atholl, Tayside; Class 47, 12.35 Inverness-Edinburgh, 23 October 1978.
As you can see, Cyril Walmesley and I are on our way from the Motorail at Perth to Granton on Spey. Although the mountains look quite threatening, the train is gradually leaving the Highlands. *10849*

Below right Dalnacardoch, Tayside; Class 47 No 47270, 13.10 Glasgow (Queen Street)-Inverness, 23 October 1978.
We are further north in Glen Garry now and, as you can observe, the up line is newly ballasted. Indeed, only a single line was intended between Blair Atholl and Dalwhinnie over the summit after rationalisation, but this proved inadequate for punctual working and double track was restored. *10854*

Above Dalwhinnie, Highland; Class 40, 14.55 Inverness-Glasgow
(Queen Street), 23 October 1978.
We've crossed the watershed and it's downhill nearly all the way to
Aviemore. The line is single track from here to Inverness with various
loops for crossing other trains. *10865*

Below Carr Bridge, Highland; Class 47, 10.35 Inverness-Euston,
'The Clansman', 24 October 1978.
Presumably the train is due to pass another here out of course, as when
we ran the saloons from Perth to Inverness (and beyond) we stopped
here and were placed in the up side of the loop to let 'The Clansman'
pass at speed on the more direct line. *10885*

Tomatin, Highland; Class 40, 12.35 Inverness-Edinburgh (Waverley), 24 October 1978.
On the far side of this fine viaduct now is a modern bridge carrying the dual-carriageway of the A9 trunk road. *10895*

Above Slochd summit, Highland; Class 40, 13.10 Glasgow (Queen Street)-Inverness, 24 October 1978.
This direct route from Aviemore to Inverness was not opened until 1897/8. *10891*

Below Invereen, Highland; Class 47, 17.35 Inverness-Glasgow (Queen Street), 24 October 1978.
This is our last illustration of the Highland line. There is still a loop to come at Moy, then double track from the Culloden Viaduct into the terminus. *10901*

Helmsdale, Highland; Class 26, 11.38 Wick/11.41 Thurso-Inverness, 9 October 1975.
I'm with Mike Cutland and we've hired a car at Dingwall, which we shall use to visit the Far North and Kyle lines, leaving it eventually at Kyle of Lochalsh to be collected and returned to base. The semaphore signals have now gone and radio-signalling substituted. When I ran the GM saloons to the Far North we had a break here on our return. It was my 50th birthday, and imagine my surprise and delight when a cake and champagne was produced in the train! *11177*

Kinbrace, Highland; Class 26, 10.50 Inverness-Wick/Thurso, 9 October 1975.
I had often seen photographers hanging out of car windows taking pictures on lines parallel to the road, and had not expected to do it myself. But here on a quiet and lonely road it was a chance to photograph isolated places not readily accessible, with Mike at the wheel and hence this shot. We were just far enough away to encompass the whole train. *11190*

Wick, Highland; Class 25, 17.33 to Inverness, 9 October 1975.
On the occasion of the saloon visit I was particularly grateful to the maintenance staff here. Repeatedly the water supplies in one of the coaches had been exhausted. We were well into lunch (from Altnabreac!) at this stage, but I left the table to seek help. One of the men took himself under the coach and found that the drain cocks had been left open to avoid freezing up. Soon all was well! *11241*

Glasgow (Queen Street), Strathclyde; Class 27, 10.00 to Edinburgh (Waverley), 14 April 1977.
Back in the Lowlands now, and this train is about to enter the tunnel and climb out of the city. Over the years many attempts have been made to speed up this inter-city service and I suspect that at this time there is another locomotive at the back giving extra impetus and enabling a quick turn-round at each end. I'm attending the AGM of National Transport Tokens Ltd, of which I was a Director. We provided the coinage for local authorities to give to deserving pensioners for reduced fares on the buses. I'm now one of them. *10129*

Above Ardlui, Strathclyde; Class 26, 08.35 Glasgow (Queen Street)-Oban, 13 May 1975.
The rest of the pictures relate to the lines to Fort William and, more especially, to Oban. On returning from our saloon trip to Glenfinnan and Oban in 1981 we had to wait here to cross a northbound service that contained youngsters returning from a football match. I stood on the platform with my after-dinner brandy – not a good example to set. *11256*

Below Inverhaggernie, Central; Class 26, up freight, 13 May 1975.
I'm standing on the open hillside in quite a cold breeze with Cyril. Later he was to catch a severe chill when similarly exposed above the Duddon Estuary in Cumbria. The train is on its way from Fort William to the Lowlands. *11265*

Above Coire Thain, Strathclyde; Class 27, freight to Fort William, 13 May 1975.
This place looks isolated, but it isn't due to the presence of the main road. We are near County March summit and the train will soon round the horseshoe bend. *11274*

Below Bridge of Orchy, Strathclyde; Class 27, 13.00 Mallaig-Glasgow (Queen Street), 13 May 1975.
This is the last station before the railway parts company with the main road, which turns to go through the Pass of Glencoe. The line heads out across the wilderness that is Rannoch Moor and will not rejoin the A82 for 50 miles. When we hired the GM saloons from Glasgow we had breakfast en route and stopped here to stretch our legs and take our pictures. *11283*

Achallader Viaduct, Strathclyde; Class 27 No 27205, southbound timber train, 13 May 1975.
This is as far as it is possible to follow the line in a normal saloon car, and then quite a walk is involved. The track from the A82 is not everyone's idea of a road. However, it was well worth while as the bleakness of Rannoch Moor is self-evident. Don't stay here too long in inclement weather... *11292*

Dalmally, Strathclyde; Class 27, 07.55 Oban-Glasgow (Queen Street), 12 May 1975.
Cyril and I are staying at a hotel in Dalmally and we've come out before breakfast to photograph this working. We shall spend much of the day – basically a wet one – between here and Oban as you will see. *11492*

Above Glenlochy, Strathclyde; Class 27 No 27019, 08.35 Glasgow (Queen Street)-Oban, 12 May 1975.
We're nearing the Pass of Brander where rock falls are indicated by a set of semaphore signals, which fall to danger when a fence of wires connected to them is broken, unless something has changed recently. *11487*

Below Loch Awe, Strathclyde; Class 27, Glasgow (Queen Street)-Oban, 12 May 1975.
Time and again this location appears in books or on TV because there are few clear places between the line and the water, and here we are on the main road bridge. *11497*

Taynuilt, Strathclyde; Class 27, Glasgow (Queen Street)-Oban, 12 May 1976.
You can see the appalling weather. I recall the first 'Royal Scotsman' excursion calling here in wonderful sunshine, and the Americans on board were invited to take a short coach tour. No one ventured out. Then one lady appeared and I said 'Good morning', at which she retreated into her seat and continued to read the *New York Herald Tribune*! *11511*

Taynuilt, Strathclyde; Class 27, 12.25 Oban-Glasgow (Queen Street), 12 May 1975.
The 'Royal Scotsman' originally consisted of a set of vintage archive coaches, and during their stay here I was able to obtain photographs of each vehicle. *11507*

Glencruitten, Strathclyde; Class 27, 17.40 Oban-Glasgow (Queen Street), 12 May 1975.
To gain Connel Ferry the line has to head south from the station at Oban and complete almost a circle to climb over the pass. *11526/11524*

Oban, Strathclyde; Class 27, 17.40 to Glasgow (Queen Street), 12 May 1975. We saw the train at the terminus before it began its ascent south of the town. Today the station has been rebuilt and is a shadow of its former self. Never mind, we have pictures to recall past glories (and probably more to come!). *11527*

INDEX

Roman numerals indicate the colour pages.